Teacher, I'm Done! Now What Do I Do ?

Written by Sue Lewis, Joellyn Cicciarelli, and Vicky Shiotsu
Editor: Christine Hood
Illustrators: Patty Briles and Jane Yamada
Cover Illustrator: Karl Edwards
Cover Designer: Barbara Peterson
Designer: Pamela Thomson
Art Director: Tom Cochrane
Project Director: Carolea Williams

Table of Contents

Introduction

Every teacher hears it from time to time—*Teacher, I'm done! Now what do I do?* Now you have the answer in this versatile, one-stop resource. *Teacher, I'm Done!* offers children the opportunity to develop knowledge, learning skills, and independence as they complete more than 80 exciting puzzles designed especially for their varied developmental levels.

Each section of this book contains fun-filled puzzles that complement one or more areas of the curriculum, including **reading, language arts, math,** and **art.**

Each puzzle offers easy-to-read directions, text supported by art, and entertaining, high-interest activities that can be completed with minimal teacher assistance. Some of the puzzles within each section are marked with a star in the top right-hand corner. These puzzles provide children with extra challenge by introducing more sophisticated tasks, higher-level concepts, and independent extension activities.

Children are guaranteed success as they work to read, follow directions, think critically and logically, and fill their spare time between assignments with lots of learning fun!

Whatever the subject area or children's developmental levels, *Teacher, I'm Done!* offers everything you need to extend learning and create constructive self-direction in your classroom. Get started today!

How to Use the Puzzles

Because young children often don't know how to constructively keep themselves busy after completing an assignment, you want to create an environment that encourages them to take initiative. This way, you are free to assist other students and work with student groups. Use the following ideas to create a "can do" situation in your classroom.

Setup and Organization

Use the pages to create activity books for each child. Duplicate selected puzzles and staple them into a "book." You can give a book to each child, or just to those children who consistently finish their work early and need an extra challenge. Children can keep the books in their desks and work at their own pace. They can also work cooperatively with partners to share solutions and find new ways of looking at problems. Place the answer key in an accessible place, so children can correct their own work.

As an alternative, create a laminated file folder for each puzzle. On the outside of each folder, attach a copy of the blank puzzle. On the left inside flap, attach a class list so children can cross out their names when they complete a puzzle. On the right inside flap, attach an answer key so children can self-correct their work before placing the completed puzzle in the folder. (Note that some pages do not need an answer key.) Be sure students go back and correct any mistakes. Place all folders in a box so children can readily access them.

To help children learn to work independently, try the following suggestions:

- When beginning each section, you may want to complete one puzzle as a class, stressing the importance of reading *all* the words on the page and observing *all* the illustrations before beginning. Show children how to carefully complete each puzzle by working slowly, thoroughly, and neatly.

- Set up a "help" system by which children can ask a buddy for assistance. Emphasize the importance of whispering and only asking buddies who have completed their original assignments as well.

Alternative Ways to Use the Puzzles

The puzzles in this resource can be used in a variety of creative and helpful ways. You can use these puzzles as:

- "sponge" activities for when you have five or ten extra minutes of transition time.

- supplemental activities that correlate with a textbook or a required element in your curriculum.

- "fun on the bus" activities as your class travels to and from field trips. Just pack clipboards with attached puzzles and pencils, and you're ready to go!

- "substitute teacher" activities if your sub has extra time.

Presto! Chango!

Name _____ Date _____

Animals

Change **dog** to **cat** by changing one letter at a time.
Use the picture clues to help you.

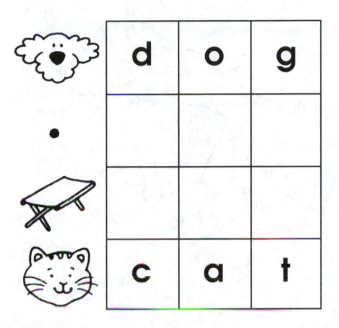

d	o	g
c	a	t

Now change **pig** to **hen**.

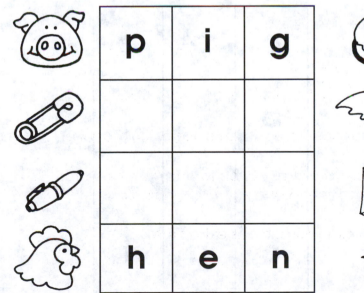

p	i	g
h	e	n

Now change **rat** to **bug**.

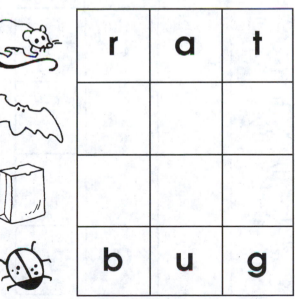

r	a	t
b	u	g

Name _____ Date _____

More Animals

Change **hen** to **ram** by changing one letter at a time.
Use the picture clues to help you.

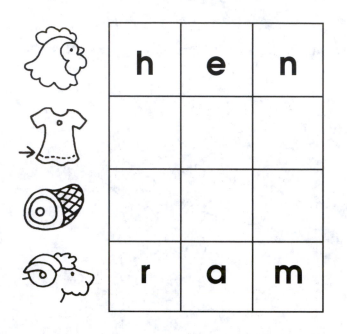

h	e	n
r	a	m

Now change **cat** to **jay**.

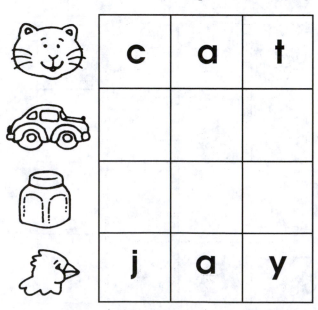

c	a	t
j	a	y

Now change **bee** to **cat**.

b	e	e
b		
c	a	t

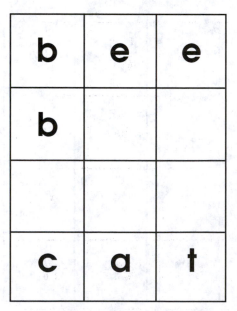

Name _____ Date _____

Transportation

Change **car** to **sub** by changing one letter at a time.
Use the picture clues to help you.

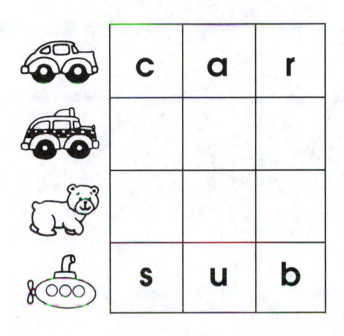

c	a	r
s	u	b

Now change **jet** to **van**.

j	e	t
	e	
		t
v	a	n

Now change **bus** to **jet**.

b	u	s
	u	
j	e	t

On the back of this paper, write three sentences.
Use a word from a puzzle in each sentence.

Name _____ Date _____

Things in the Kitchen

Change **nut** to **ham** by changing one letter at a time.
Use the picture clues to help you.

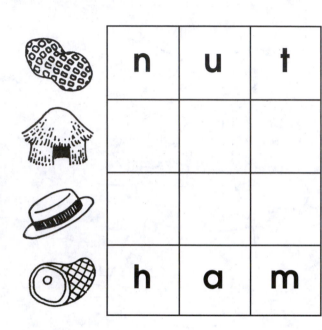

n	u	t
h	a	m

Now change **jar** to **pan**.   Now change **mat** to **rug**.

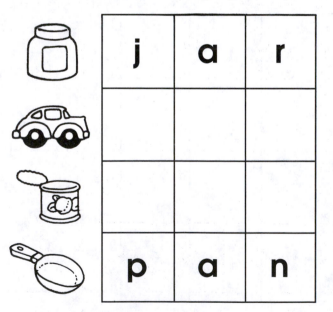

j	a	r
p	a	n

m	a	t
		g
r	u	g

On the back of this paper, write three sentences.
Use a word from a puzzle in each sentence.

Teacher, I'm Done! ©2001 Creative Teaching Press

Name _____ Date _____

Silent e Words

Change **hive** to **tire** by changing one letter at a time.
Use the picture clues to help you.

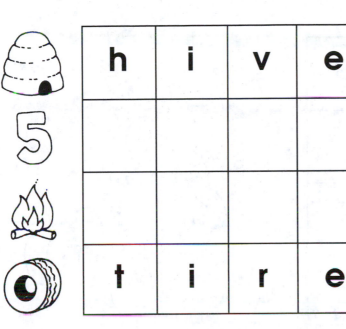

h	i	v	e
t	i	r	e

Now change **robe** to **hole**.

r	o	b	e
h	o	l	e

Now change **gate** to **cake**.

g	a	t	e
		m	
c	a	k	e

On the back of this paper, write 10 new silent e words.

Name _____ Date _____

More Silent *e* Words

Change **bike** to **cape** by changing one letter at a time.
Use the picture clues to help you.

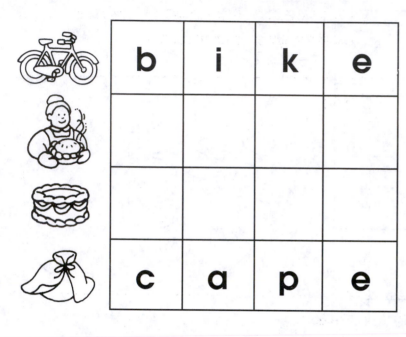

b	i	k	e
c	a	p	e

Now change **cave** to **bone**.

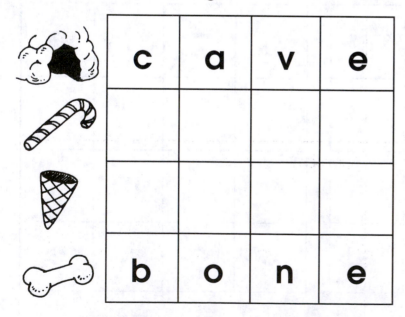

c	a	v	e
b	o	n	e

Now change **take** to **rice**.

t	a	k	e
		k	
r	i	c	e

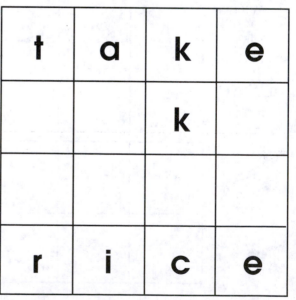

On the back of this paper, write a sentence using at least three silent *e* words from the puzzles.

Name _____ Date _____

Artsy Adjectives

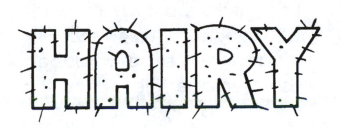

Look at the word *hairy*. It is written with special letters to show its meaning. Write the words below. Use special letters to show the meaning of each word.

tiny	thin
sharp	wide
fat	rocky

Name _____   Date _____

More Artsy Adjectives

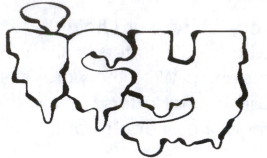

Look at the word *icy*. It is written with special letters to show its meaning. Write the words below. Use special letters to show the meaning of each word.

bumpy	hot
flat	**spotted**
fancy	**dirty**

On the back of this paper, write more "artsy adjectives" using special letters.

Name _____ Date _____

Nifty Nouns

Look at the word *fire*. It is written with special letters to show its meaning. Write the words below. Use special letters to show the meaning of each word.

rain	grass
smoke	**chain**
rope	**snow**

Teacher, I'm Done! ©2001 Creative Teaching Press

Name _____ Date _____

More Nifty Nouns

Look at the word *garden*. It is written with special letters to show its meaning. Write the words below. Use special letters to show the meaning of each word.

shadow	cloud
ribbon	**forest**
cat	**mountain**

On the back of this paper, write more "nifty nouns" using special letters.

Name _____ Date _____

Visual Verbs

double
double (reflected/upside-down)

Look at the word **double**. It is written with special letters to show its meaning. Write the words below. Use special letters to show the meaning of each word.

freeze	**twist**
slant	**drip**
split	**fall**

Name _____ Date _____

More Visual Verbs

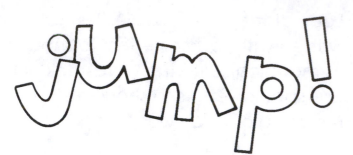

Look at the word *jump*. It is written with special letters to show its meaning. Write the words below. Use special letters to show the meaning of each word.

wiggle	**rip**
smile	**run**
stretch	**squish**

On the back of this paper, write more "visual verbs" using special letters.

Name _____ Date _____

Goat's Clues

Fill in the missing letters to make words that have *oat* in them. Use the picture clues to help you.

g o a t

1. | | o | a | t |

2. | | o | a | t |

3. | | o | a | t |

4. | | | | o | a | t |

5. | | | o | a | t |

On the back of this paper, write a sentence using two of the *oat* words above.

Name _____ Date _____

Kitty's Clues

Use the letters in the word *cat*
to complete each word below.
Use the picture clues to help you.

1.  | c | a | r | t |

2.  | | o | | |

3.  | | | | k |

4. 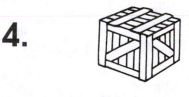 | | r | | | e |

5. 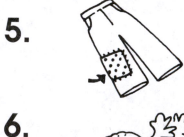 | p | | | | h |

6.  | | | r | r | o | |

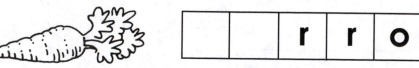 On the back of this paper, write a sentence using
two of the *cat* words above.

Name _____ Date _____

Bunny's Clues

Fill in the missing letters to make words that have **ear** in them. Use the clues to help you.

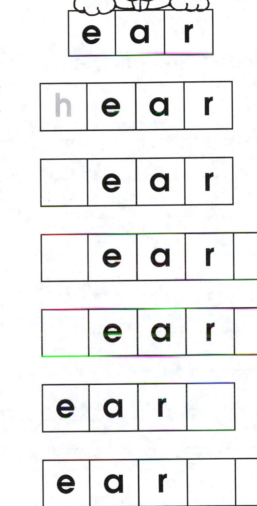

1. what ears do

h	e	a	r

2. to be afraid

	e	a	r

3. they fall when you cry

	e	a	r	

4. pumps blood in your body

	e	a	r	

5. to make money from working

e	a	r	

6. not late

e	a	r		

7. the planet we live on

e	a	r		

8. what teachers help you do

	e	a	r	

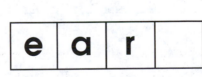

On the back of this paper, write at least three other words that have **ear** in them.

Name _____ Date _____

Trick or Treat

Use the letters in the sentence below to make as many new words as you can. Write them on the lines. Read the examples to help you get started.

What is your favorite trick or treat, and why?

was _____   _____

try _____   _____

_____   _____

_____   _____

_____   _____

_____   _____

_____   _____

_____   _____

On the back of this paper, write an answer to the question.

Name _____ Date _____

Giving Thanks

Use the letters in the sentence below to make as many new words as you can. Write them on the lines. Read the examples to help you get started.

What good things are you most thankful for?

moon _____   _____

hare _____   _____

_____   _____

_____   _____

_____   _____

_____   _____

_____   _____

_____   _____

_____   _____

On the back of this paper, write an answer to the question.

Name _____ Date _____

Winter Wonders

Use the letters in the sentence below to make as many new words as you can. Write them on the lines.

What do you like to do in the winter?

_____ _____

_____ _____

_____ _____

_____ _____

_____ _____

_____ _____

_____ _____

_____ _____

On the back of this paper, write an answer to the question.

Name _____ Date _____

Be My Valentine

Use the letters in the sentence below to make as many new words as you can. Write them on the lines.

Who is your favorite Valentine?

_____   _____

_____   _____

_____   _____

_____   _____

_____   _____

_____   _____

_____   _____

_____   _____

On the back of this paper, write an answer to the question.

Name _____ Date _____

Fun in the Sun

Use the letters in the sentence below to make as many new words as you can. Write them on the lines.

What is summer fun?

_____   _____

_____   _____

_____   _____

_____   _____

_____   _____

_____   _____

_____   _____

_____   _____

On the back of this paper, write an answer to the question.

Name _____ Date _____

Add It Up!

There are 12 addition problems in the puzzle. Circle them.
They can go across or down.

Hint: A number can be used in more than one problem.

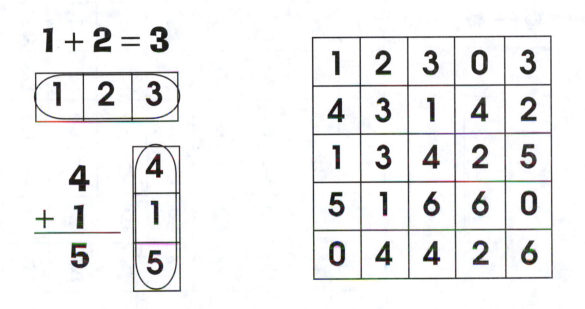

$$1 + 2 = 3$$

1	2	3

$$\begin{array}{r} 4 \\ + 1 \\ \hline 5 \end{array}$$

4
1
5

1	2	3	0	3
4	3	1	4	2
1	3	4	2	5
5	1	6	6	0
0	4	4	2	6

On the back of this paper, write all the problems you found.

Name _____ Date _____

The Sum of It

There are 18 addition problems in the puzzle. Circle them.
They can go across or down.

Hint: A number can be used in more than one problem.

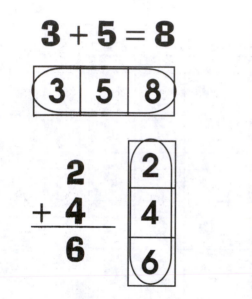

2	6	8	0	4	3	7	9
4	1	8	9	2	7	9	3
6	2	4	9	1	2	3	0
2	5	7	1	8	9	2	3
8	2	9	0	3	8	0	2
6	7	6	1	7	4	2	5

On the back of this paper, write all the problems you found.

Name _____ Date _____

Really "Sum-thing"!

There are 32 addition problems in the puzzle. Circle them.
They can go across or down.

Hint: A number can be used in more than one problem.

$$8 + 4 = 12$$

(8	4	12)

$$\begin{array}{r} 9 \\ + 2 \\ \hline 11 \end{array}$$

8	6	14	3	2	9	11	6
1	7	1	6	7	1	6	7
9	6	15	9	9	18	17	13
0	13	13	3	16	1	6	2
4	4	8	12	7	19	8	5
1	17	18	2	7	7	14	7
5	14	3	8	11	6	0	4
15	6	4	10	18	1	7	8

On the back of this paper, make your own addition puzzle.
Ask a friend to solve it.

Name _____ Date _____

Subract It!

There are 11 subtraction problems in the puzzle. Circle them.
They can go across or down.

Hint: A number can be used in more than one problem.

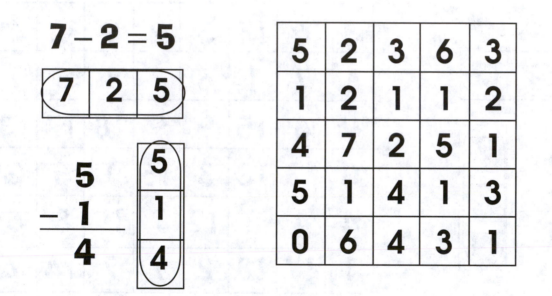

5	2	3	6	3
1	2	1	1	2
4	7	2	5	1
5	1	4	1	3
0	6	4	3	1

On the back of this paper, write all the problems you found.

Name _____ Date _____

Find the Difference

There are 15 subtraction problems in the puzzle. Circle them.
They can go across or down.

Hint: A number can be used in more than one problem.

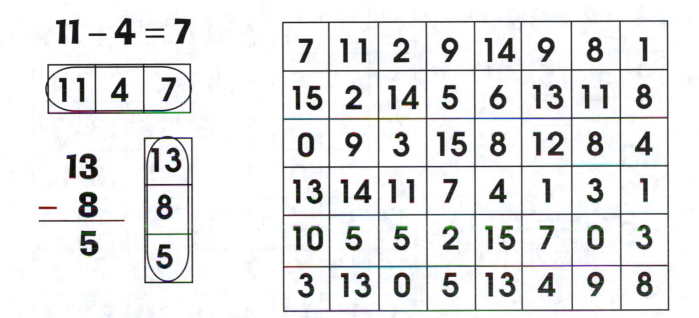

7	11	2	9	14	9	8	1
15	2	14	5	6	13	11	8
0	9	3	15	8	12	8	4
13	14	11	7	4	1	3	1
10	5	5	2	15	7	0	3
3	13	0	5	13	4	9	8

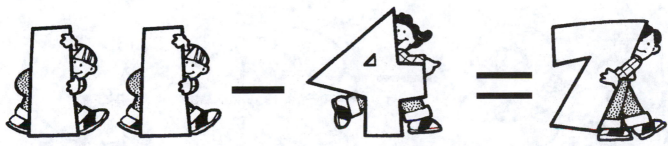

 On the back of this paper, write all the problems you found.

Name _____ Date _____

More Minuses

There are 24 subtraction problems in the puzzle. Circle them.
They can go across or down.

Hint: A number can be used in more than one problem.

$$19 - 4 = 15$$

| 19 | 4 | 15 |

$$\begin{array}{r} 18 \\ -\ 9 \\ \hline 9 \end{array}$$

18
9
9

17	6	11	6	11	13	2	11
5	16	8	8	17	5	14	4
12	7	5	1	3	18	13	7
16	7	0	7	14	1	13	18
16	9	5	4	16	17	2	12
15	13	6	7	1	6	11	6
1	13	12	0	15	10	5	6
14	0	15	3	12	12	15	8

On the back of this paper, make your own subtraction puzzle.
Ask a friend to solve it.

Name _____ Date _____

Four Square

Look at the number puzzle. Read the positions of the numbers to fill in and solve the problems below.

$$\frac{1\ |\ 2}{3\ |\ 4}$$

Hint: $\llcorner$ = 1

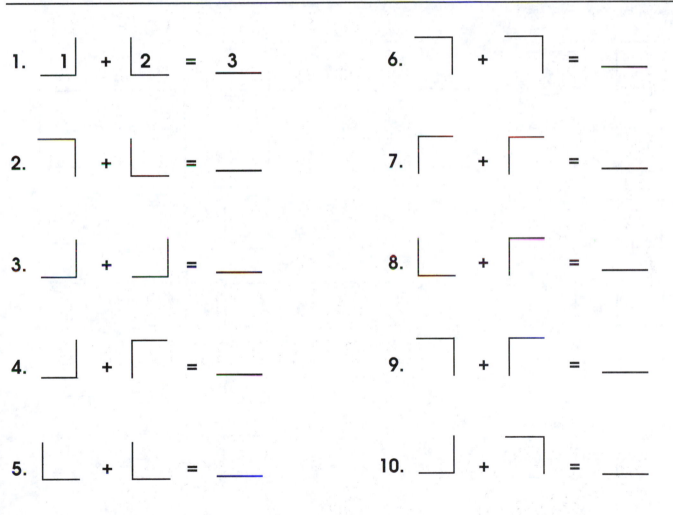

1. $\underline{\ \ 1\ |}$ + $|\ 2\ $ = $\underline{\ \ 3\ \ }$

2. $\overline{\ \ |}$ + $\underline{\ }$ = $\underline{\ \ \ }$

3. $\underline{\ |}$ + $\underline{\ |}$ = $\underline{\ \ }$

4. $\underline{\ }$ + $\overline{|\ }$ = $\underline{\ \ }$

5. $\llcorner$ + $\llcorner$ = $\underline{\ \ }$

6. $\overline{\ }\ $ + $\overline{\ }\ $ = $\underline{\ \ }$

7. $\overline{\ |}$ + $\overline{\ |}$ = $\underline{\ \ }$

8. $\llcorner$ + $\overline{\ |}$ = $\underline{\ \ }$

9. $\overline{\ }\ $ + $\overline{\ |}$ = $\underline{\ \ }$

10. $\underline{\ }\ $ + $\overline{\ }\ $ = $\underline{\ \ }$

On the back of this paper, write three new problems for the "four square" puzzle.

Teacher, I'm Done! ©2001 Creative Teaching Press

Name _____ Date _____

Six Square

Look at the number puzzle.
Read the positions of the
numbers to fill in and solve
the problems below.

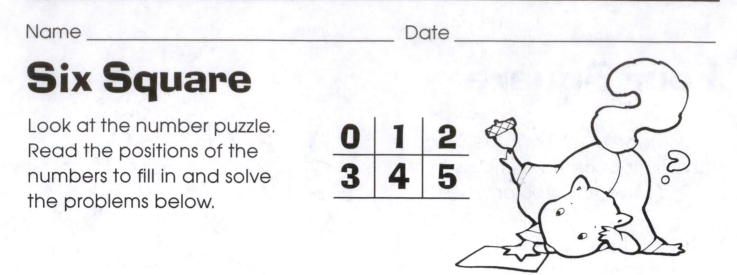

0	1	2
3	4	5

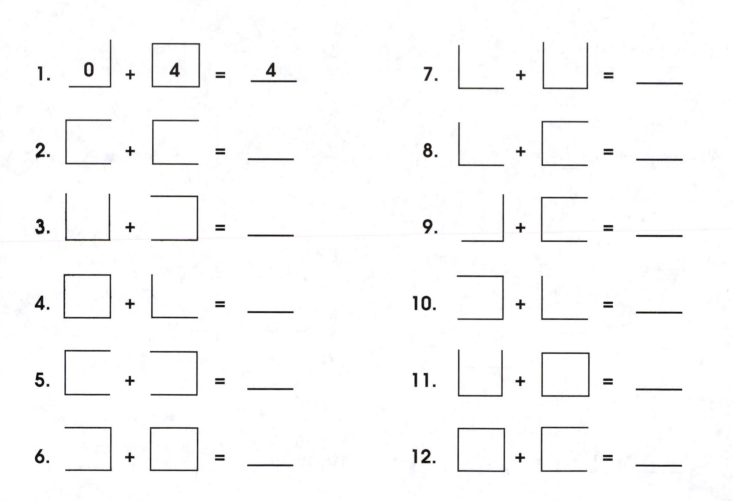

1. $0 + 4 = 4$

2. __ + __ = __

3. __ + __ = __

4. __ + __ = __

5. __ + __ = __

6. __ + __ = __

7. __ + __ = __

8. __ + __ = __

9. __ + __ = __

10. __ + __ = __

11. __ + __ = __

12. __ + __ = __

On the back of this paper, write three new problems
for the "six square" puzzle.

Name _____ Date _____

Nine Square

Look at the number puzzle. Read the positions of the numbers to fill in and solve the problems below.

5	2	7
3	8	9
6	1	4

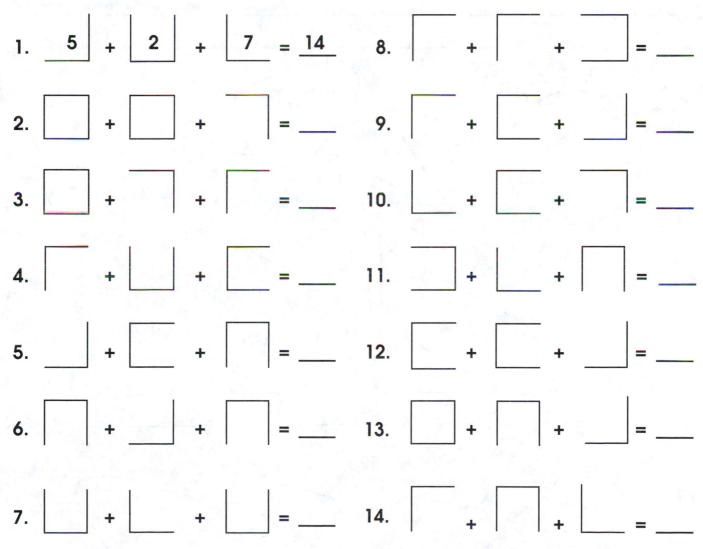

1. [5] + [2] + [7] = 14   8. ☐ + ☐ + ☐ = ___

2. ☐ + ☐ + ☐ = ___   9. ☐ + ☐ + ☐ = ___

3. ☐ + ☐ + ☐ = ___   10. ☐ + ☐ + ☐ = ___

4. ☐ + ☐ + ☐ = ___   11. ☐ + ☐ + ☐ = ___

5. ☐ + ☐ + ☐ = ___   12. ☐ + ☐ + ☐ = ___

6. ☐ + ☐ + ☐ = ___   13. ☐ + ☐ + ☐ = ___

7. ☐ + ☐ + ☐ = ___   14. ☐ + ☐ + ☐ = ___

On the back of this paper, write three new problems for the "nine square" puzzle.

Name _____ Date _____

Sail Away

Use the color key to color the picture below.

Color Key		
1, one, • = blue	4, four, = yellow	
2, two, •• = red	5, five, = orange	
3, three, ••• = green	6, six, = purple	

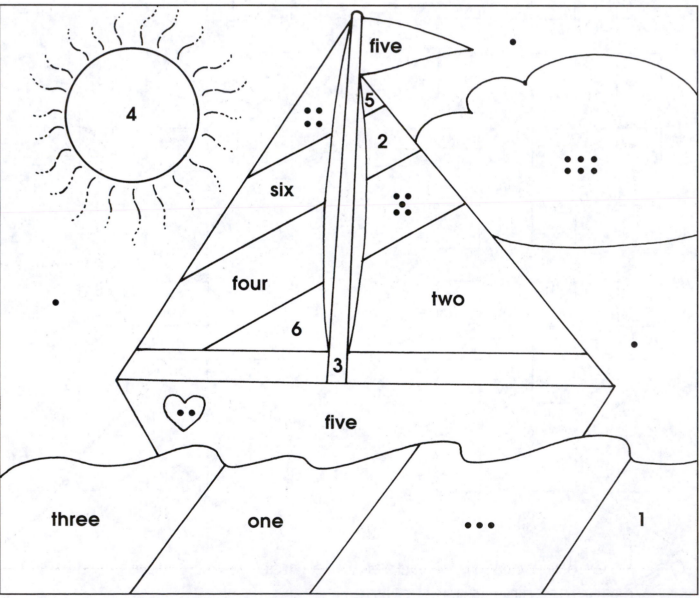

Name _____ Date _____

Bee Happy!

Color the even numbers less than 16 **yellow**.
Color the even numbers more than 16 **purple**.
Color the odd numbers less than 15 **brown**.
Color the odd numbers more than 15 **orange**.

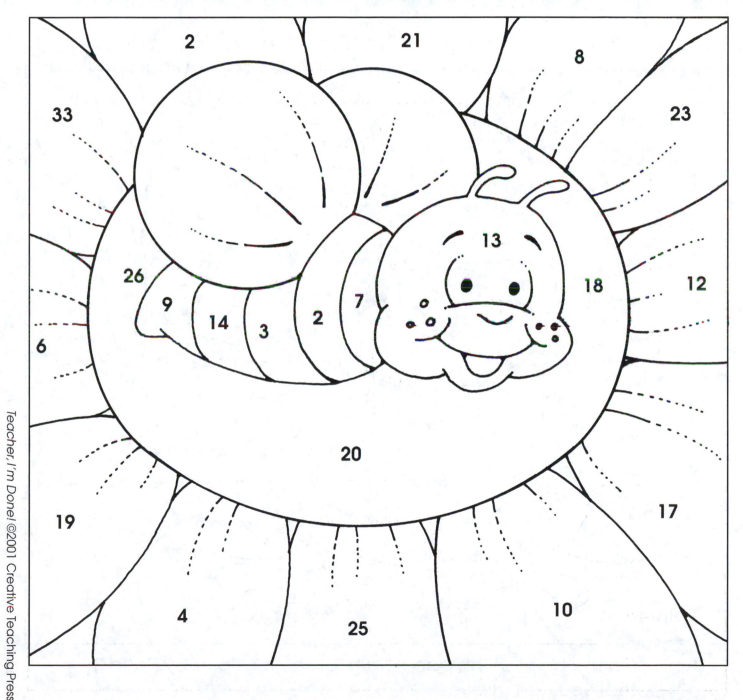

Name _____ Date _____

Funny Frog

Color the multiples of 2 green.
Color the multiples of 3 blue.
Use any color to color the spaces without numbers.

On the back of this paper, write all the multiples of 2 and 3 that you can think of.

Name _____ Date _____

Write the Number

Write the number words
for 1 to 12 to fill in the
puzzle. Use the word
bank to help you.

Word Bank	
1	2
one	two
3	4
three	four
5	6
five	six
7	8
seven	eight
9	10
nine	ten
11	12
eleven	twelve

Name _____ Date _____

Add and Write

Solve each addition problem. Write the answers in number words to fill in the puzzle.

Across

1. 6 + 6 = ___
2. 5 + 4 = ___
5. 13 + 5 = ___

Down

1. 7 + 6 = ___
3. 3 + 4 = ___
4. 5 + 6 = ___

6. 6 + 2 = ___
7. 15 + 5 = ___
8. 0 + 1 = ___

9. 11 + 8 = ___

Make your own addition crossword on graph paper. Be sure it has at least seven problems. Ask a friend to solve it.

Name _____ Date _____

Subtract and Write

Solve each subtraction problem. Write the answers in number words to fill in the puzzle.

Across

2. 12 − 4 = ___
3. 16 − 2 = ___
4. 15 − 8 = ___
6. 19 − 18 = ___
9. 25 − 14 = ___
10. 16 − 14 = ___

Down

1. 15 − 5 = ___
4. 20 − 14 = ___
5. 8 − 5 = ___
7. 18 − 9 = ___
8. 17 − 8 = ___
11. 29 − 28 = ___

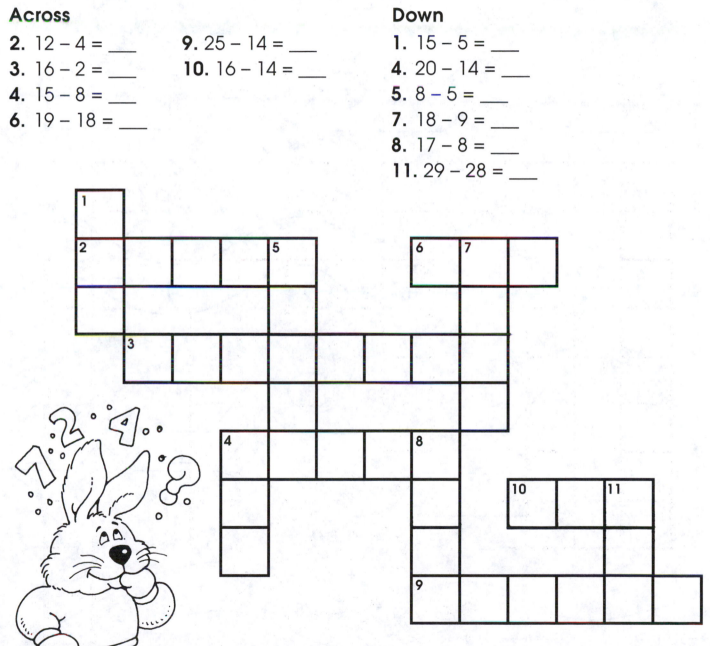

Teacher, I'm Done! ©2001 Creative Teaching Press

Make your own subtraction crossword on graph paper. Be sure it has at least seven problems. Ask a friend to solve it.

Name _____ Date _____

Desert Trail

Follow the path of numbers on each trail. How do the numbers fit a pattern? Write numbers on the lines to complete each pattern. Then write the "pattern rule." The first one is done for you.

1. 3 4 5 6 7 8 9 10 11 12 13

Rule: +1

2. 4 6 ___ 10 12 ___ 16 ___ 20

Rule: _____

3. 3 6 ___ 12 15 ___ 21 ___

Rule: _____

4. 5 10 ___ 20 25 ___ 35 ___

Rule: _____

Name _____ Date _____

Hiking Trail

Follow the path of numbers on each trail. How do the numbers fit a pattern? Write numbers on the lines to complete each pattern. Then write the "pattern rule."

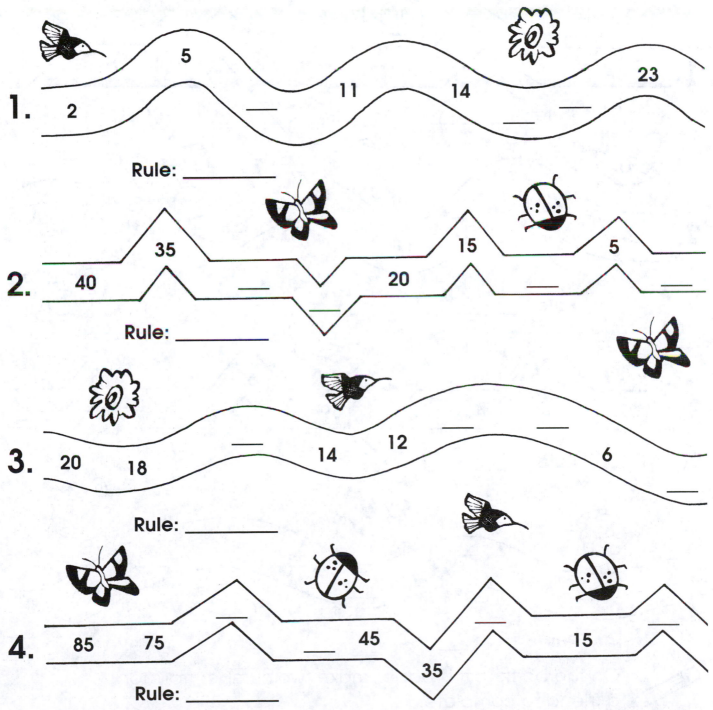

1. 2 5 ___ 11 14 ___ 23

Rule: _____

2. 40 35 ___ ___ 20 15 ___ 5 ___

Rule: _____

3. 20 18 ___ 14 12 ___ 6 ___

Rule: _____

4. 85 75 ___ ___ 45 35 ___ 15 ___

Rule: _____

Teacher, I'm Done! ©2001 Creative Teaching Press

Name _____ Date _____

Pet Paths

Follow the path of numbers on each trail. How do the numbers fit a pattern? Write numbers on the lines to complete each pattern. Then write the "pattern rule."

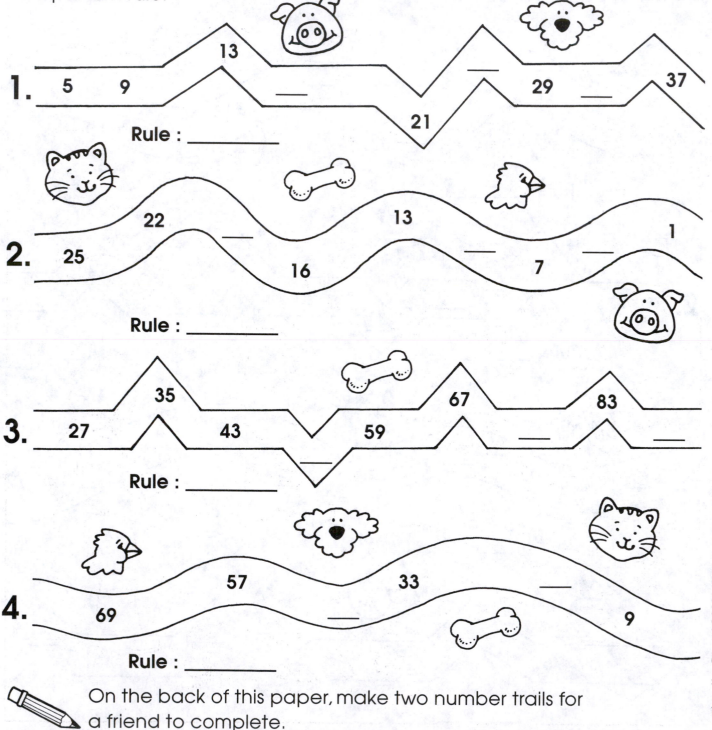

1. 5   9   13   ___   21   ___   29   ___   37

Rule : _____

2. 25   22   ___   16   13   ___   7   ___   1

Rule : _____

3. 27   35   43   ___   59   67   ___   83   ___

Rule : _____

4. 69   57   ___   33   ___   9

Rule : _____

On the back of this paper, make two number trails for a friend to complete.

Name _____ Date _____

Time for Recess

Look carefully at the picture. Circle 10 "mistakes." One is done for you.

Name _____   Date _____

Max's Messy Room

Look carefully at the picture. Circle 15 "mistakes." One is done for you.

Teacher, I'm Done! ©2001 Creative Teaching Press

Name _____ Date _____

Toy Store

Look carefully at the picture. Circle 20 "mistakes." One is done for you.

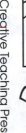 On the back of this paper, draw a picture with 10 "mistakes." Ask a friend to find and circle the mistakes.

Name _____ Date _____

Sports Fan

Circle the picture in each group that does not belong. Color the pictures that go together.

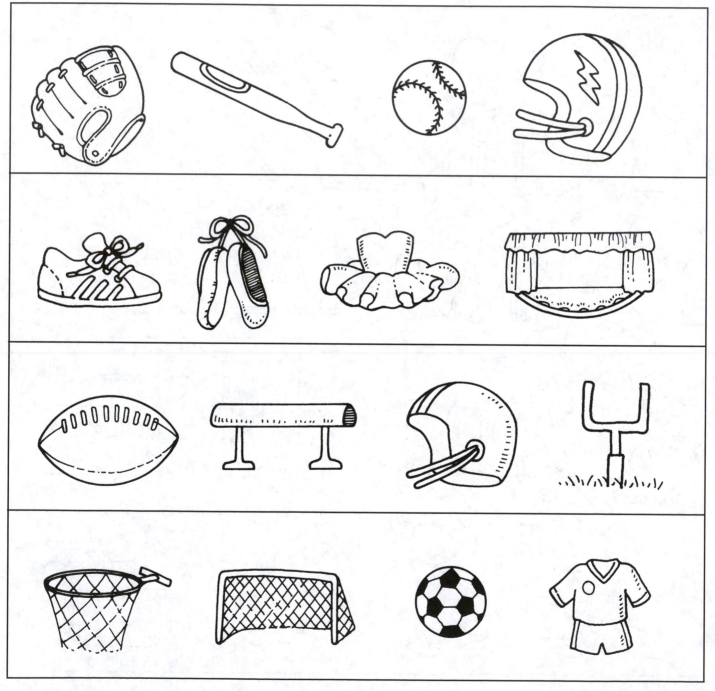

On the back of this paper, draw a picture of yourself playing your favorite sport.

Name _____   Date _____

Get in Shape

Circle the picture in each group that does not belong. Color the pictures that go together.

On the back of this paper, draw a picture of three objects with the same shape.

Name _____ Date _____

Think About It!

Circle the word in each group that does not belong.

red blue white square	big little boy tall	hand long face leg	June Monday March May	dirt tree flower plant
tree leaf trunk water	candy cookies apple cake	dog cow cat bug	apple milk banana orange	candy milk water tea
whale fish boat shark	big girl boy man	horse bird duck goose	car truck bus skates	blue red dark green

Choose a box from above. On the back of this paper, draw a picture of the three words that go together. Then write *why* they go together.

Name _____ Date _____

Behind the Curtain

Look at the **bold** words in each row.
Find the letter that is in the first two
words, but not in the third word.
Write the letter on the line.

When you are done, read the letters
from top to bottom to find out what
is behind the curtain!

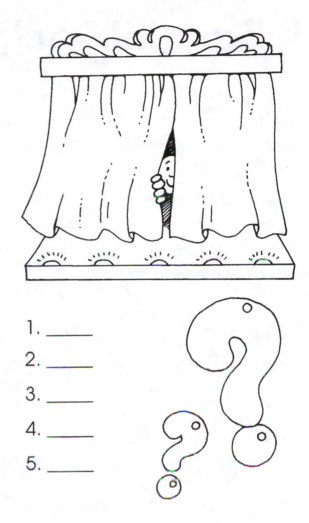

1. It's in **hat** and **wish**, but not in **bug**.

2. It's in **cot** and **rod**, but not in **Sam**.

3. It's in **jar** and **rug**, but not in **fun**.

4. It's in **is** and **sat**, but not in **mug**.

5. It's in **egg** and **Ben**, but not in **jam**.

1. _____

2. _____

3. _____

4. _____

5. _____

Draw a picture of the answer below.

Teacher, I'm Done! ©2001 Creative Teaching Press

Name _____ Date _____

A Special Package

Look at the **bold** words in each row. Find the letter that is in the first two words, but not in the third word. Write the letter on the line.

When you are done, read the letters from top to bottom to find out what kind of toy is in the package!

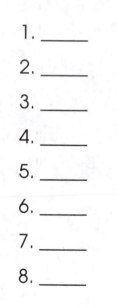

1. It's in **first** and **second**, but not in **third**.   1. _____

2. It's in **hawk** and **goat**, but not in **deer**.   2. _____

3. It's in **dime** and **nickel**, but not in **penny**.   3. _____

4. It's in **hill** and **lake**, but not in **river**.   4. _____

5. It's in **blue** and **brown**, but not in **red**.   5. _____

6. It's in **cool** and **hot**, but not in **warm**.   6. _____

7. It's in **sand** and **crab**, but not in **shell**.   7. _____

8. It's in **kite** and **top**, but not in **ball**.   8. _____

Draw a picture of the toy below.

Teacher, I'm Done! ©2001 Creative Teaching Press

Name _____ Date _____

In the Sky

Look at the **bold** words in each row. Find the letter that is in the first two words, but not in the third word. Write the letter on the line.

When you are done, read the letters from top to bottom to find out what is in the night sky.

1. It's in **Mars** and **moon**, but not in **planet**.
2. It's in **Venus** and **comet**, but not in **sky**.
3. It's in **Earth** and **dust**, but not in **nebula**.
4. It's in **Jupiter** and **oxygen**, but not in **gas**.
5. It's in **asteroid** and **Pluto**, but not in **star**.
6. It's in **ray** and **Saturn**, but not in **space**.

1. ____
2. ____
3. ____
4. ____
5. ____
6. ____

Draw a picture of the answer below.

Name _____ Date _____

Pat's Cats

These are Pat's cats. They all have one thing in common.

These are not Pat's cats. They do not have what Pat's cats have.

Find Pat's cats. Circle them.

On the back of this paper, draw one of Pat's cats.

Name _____ Date _____

The Blobs

These are Blobs from Planet Org. They all have two things in common.

These are not Blobs. They do not have the same two things the Blobs have.

Find three Blobs. Circle them.

 On the back of this paper, draw some Blobs.

Name _____ Date _____

Awesome Aces

These are Awesome Aces. They all have three things in common.

These are not Awesome Aces. They do not have the same three things the Awesome Aces have.

Find three Awesome Aces. Circle them.

 On the back of this paper, draw your own Awesome Ace. Describe what makes it awesome.

54 Critical Thinking/Logic

Name _____ Date _____

Happy Apples

Below are four pairs of apples that are exactly alike. Draw a line between each matching pair. Then circle the apple without a partner.

 On the back of this paper, draw a partner for the apple without a match.

Name _____ Date _____

Crazy Cows

Below are five pairs of cows that are exactly alike. Draw a line between each matching pair. Then circle the cow without a partner.

On the back of this paper, draw a partner for the cow without a match.

Name _____ Date _____

Tricky Totems

Below are five pairs of totem poles that are exactly alike. Draw a line between each matching pair. Then circle the totem pole without a partner.

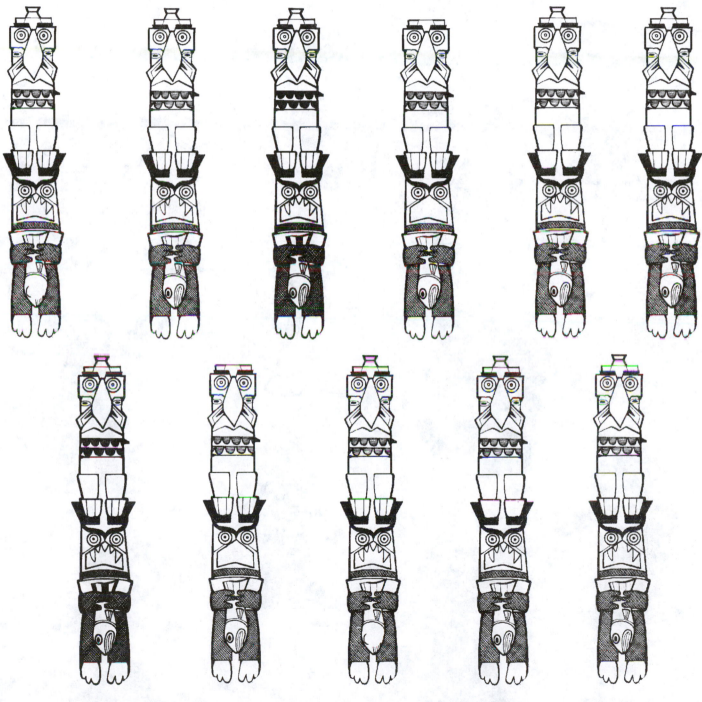

On the back of this paper, draw a partner for the totem pole without a match.

Teacher, I'm Done! ©2001 Creative Teaching Press

Name _____ Date _____

Find the Partners

Draw a line from each child to his or her shadow.

Name _____ Date _____

Flipped Partners

Draw a line from each child to his or her shadow.

Name _____ Date _____

Shadow to Shadow

Draw a line from each monkey's shadow to its match.

What would your shadow look like?
Draw your shadow on the back of this paper.

Name _____ Date _____

Ice Cream Dream

Draw the other half of the ice-cream cone. Color your picture.

Name _____ Date _____

Flower Fantasy

Draw the other half of the flower. Color your picture.

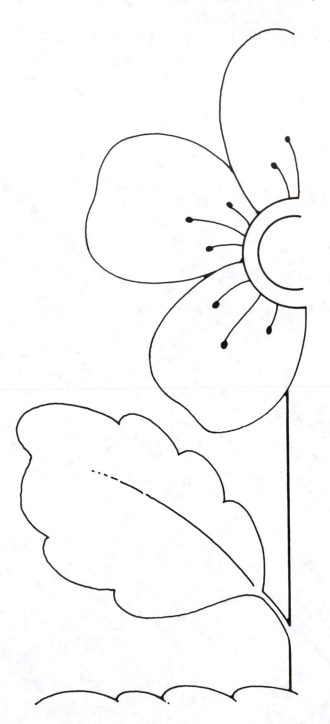

Teacher, I'm Done! ©2001 Creative Teaching Press

Name _____ Date _____

Beautiful Butterfly

Draw the other half of the butterfly. Color your picture.

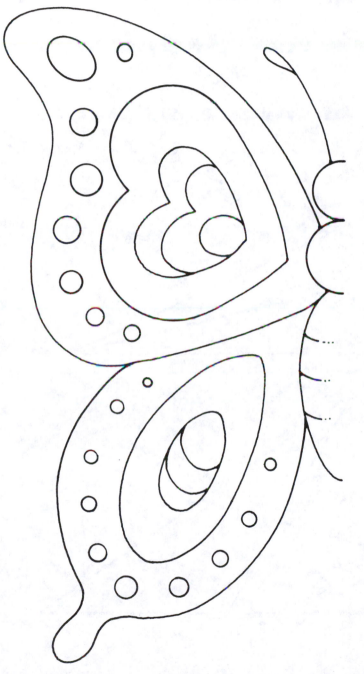

Draw a "half picture" on the back of this paper.
Ask a friend to finish it.

Counting Triangles

How many triangles are in each shape?

Hint: Two or more small triangles can be shaped like a bigger triangle.

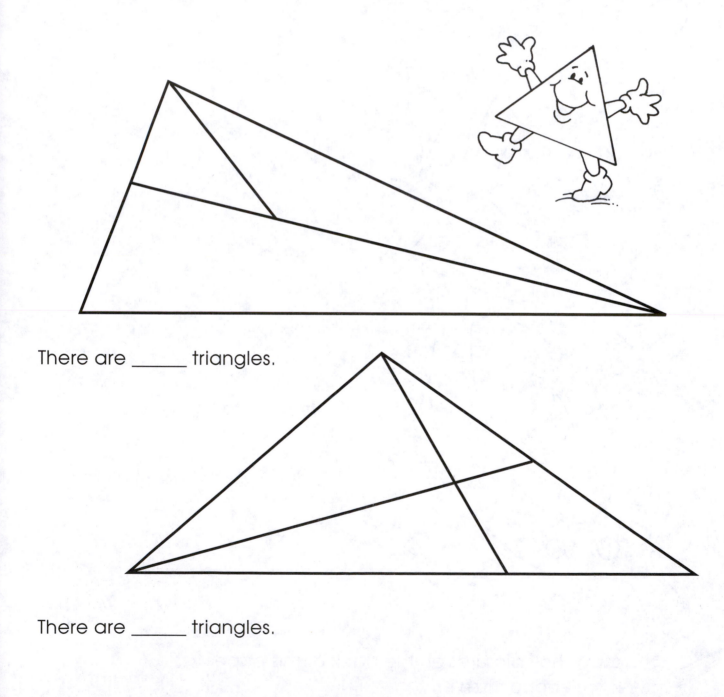

There are _____ triangles.

There are _____ triangles.

Name _____ Date _____

Counting Squares

How many squares are in each shape?

Hint: Two or more small squares can be shaped
like a bigger square.

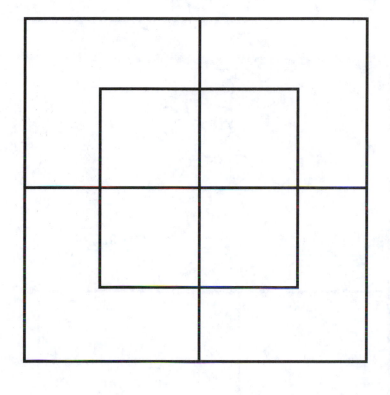

There are _____ squares.

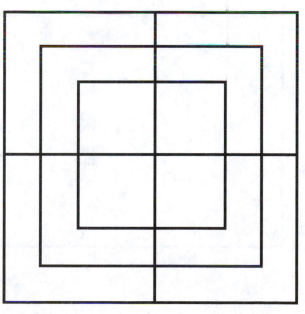

There are _____ squares.

Teacher, I'm Done! ©2001 Creative Teaching Press

Using only squares, draw a picture on the back of this paper.

Name _____ Date _____

Counting Rectangles

How many rectangles are in this shape?

Hint: Two or more small rectangles can be shaped like a bigger rectangle.

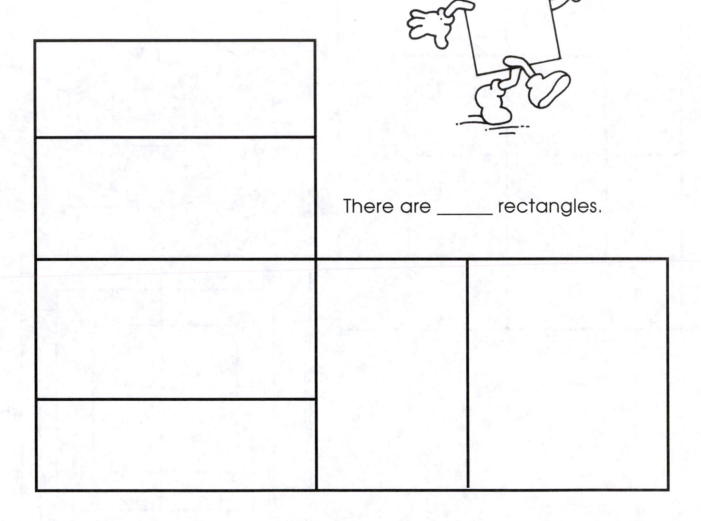

There are _____ rectangles.

On the back of this paper, draw your own shape puzzle. Ask a friend to solve it.

Name _____ Date _____

Square Dare

Use a pencil or crayon to turn each
square into a picture.

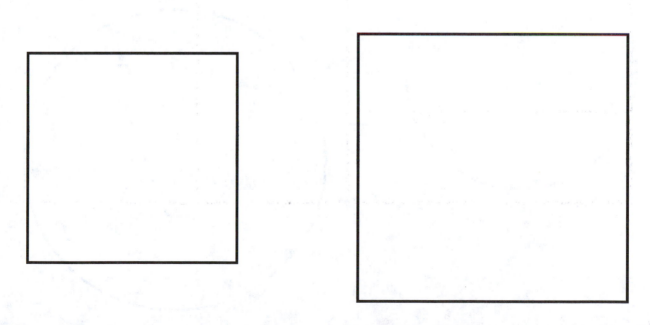

Draw more square pictures on the back of this paper.

Name _____ Date _____

Circle Works

Use a pencil or crayon to turn each circle into a picture.

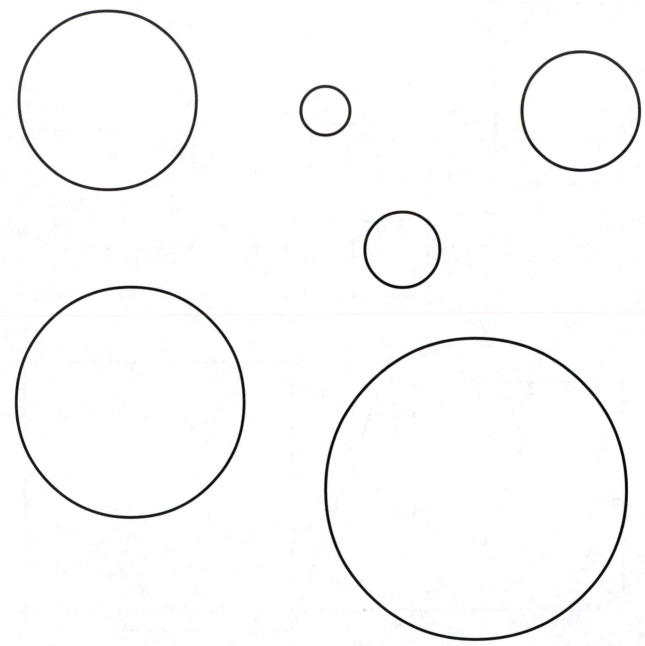

 Draw more circle pictures on the back of this paper.

Teacher, I'm Done! ©2001 Creative Teaching Press

Name _____ Date _____

Triangle Tricks

Use a pencil or crayon to turn each triangle into a picture.

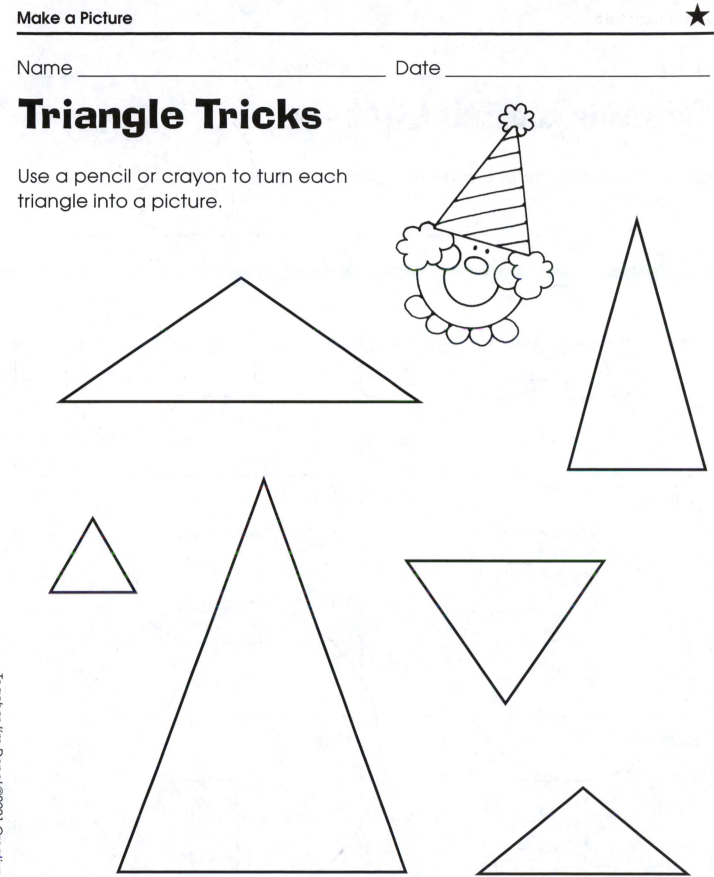

Where do you see triangles around you?
Write a list on the back of this paper.

Name _____ Date _____

Drawing with Letters

Change each letter into a picture of the word above it.

Alien	Boy
A	B
Cat	**Dog**
C	D
Elephant	**Flower**
E	F

Name _____ Date _____

Lovely Letters

Change each letter into something whose name begins with that letter.

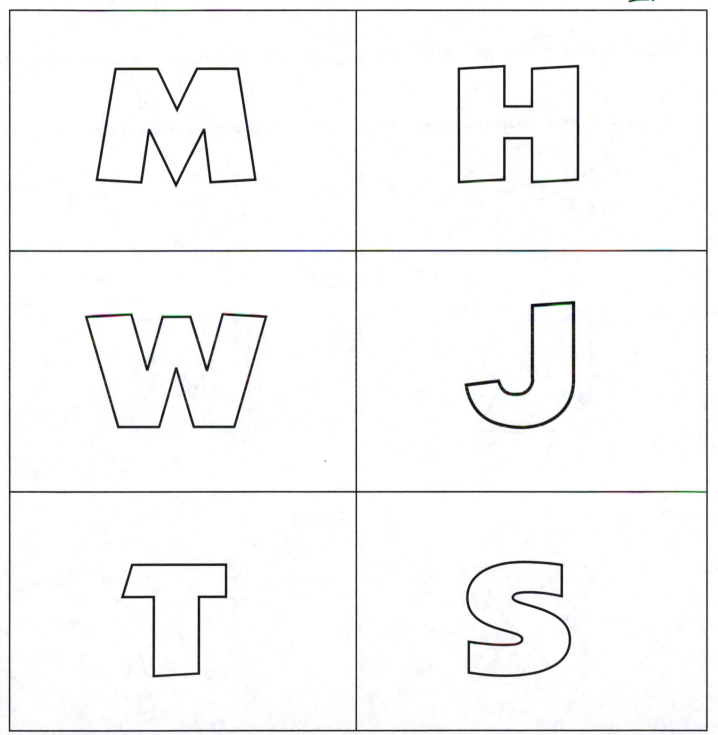

Name _____ Date _____

More Lovely Letters

Change each letter into something whose name begins with that letter.

Teacher, I'm Done! ©2001 Creative Teaching Press

Name _____ Date _____

Bounty of Bowls

How many ways can you use a bowl?

On the left side of the paper, write real uses for a bowl. On the right side, write pretend uses for a bowl. Read the examples to help you get started.

Real Uses

to hold soup

_____

_____

_____

_____

_____

_____

_____

_____

_____

Pretend Uses

as a hat

_____

_____

_____

_____

_____

_____

_____

_____

_____

Name _____   Date _____

My Cool Chair

What could you add to this
chair to make it really cool?
A motor and wheels? A soda
cooler? What else?

Write as many ideas as you can think of below.

_____   _____

_____   _____

_____   _____

_____   _____

_____   _____

_____   _____

_____   _____

_____   _____

_____   _____

On the back of this paper, draw a picture of your new cool chair.

Name _____ Date _____

Hangin' Around

Pretend that you could bend and twist a
hanger into any shape you like. What
could you use the hanger for? As a frame
for a kite? As a plant hook?

Write as many ideas as you can think of below.

_____   _____

_____   _____

_____   _____

_____   _____

_____   _____

_____   _____

_____   _____

_____   _____

_____   _____

On the back of this paper, draw a picture of a favorite
idea from your list.

Name _____ Date _____

Comparing Pets

How are cats and dogs alike? How are they different? Write as many ideas as you can think of below.

Alike

_____

_____

_____

_____

_____

_____

_____

_____

_____

_____

_____

Different

_____

_____

_____

_____

_____

_____

_____

_____

_____

_____

_____

On the back of this paper, draw a picture of a favorite dog or cat you know.

Name _____ Date _____

Lots of Light

Think about a lamp and the sun. How are they alike? How are they different?

Write as many ideas as you can think of below.

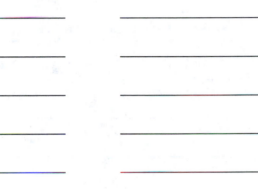

Alike

_____

_____

_____

_____

_____

_____

_____

_____

_____

Different

_____

_____

_____

_____

_____

_____

_____

_____

_____

On the back of this paper, draw what you like to do on a sunny day.

Teacher, I'm Done! ©2001 Creative Teaching Press

★

Name _____ Date _____

Get the Scoop

Think about a spoon and a dump truck.
How are they alike? How are they different?

Write as many ideas as you can think
of below.

Alike

_____

_____

_____

_____

_____

_____

_____

_____

_____

_____

Different

_____

_____

_____

_____

_____

_____

_____

_____

_____

_____

On the back of this paper, write all the different ways you can
use a spoon. Use your imagination!

Name _____ Date _____

Mike's Market

Look at the map below. There are three paths marked from Mia's house to Mike's Market. Which way is shortest? Use a ruler to measure each route. Trace the shortest way with a crayon.

About how many inches is the shortest route? _____

Name _____ Date _____

Field Trip Fun

Look at the map and read the directions. To find out where Ms. Garcia's class went on their field trip, trace the path with a crayon.

1. Start at the school parking lot.
2. Turn left out of the parking lot.
3. Turn right on Elm Street.
4. Turn left on State Street.
5. Pass three lights.
6. Turn left into the first parking lot.

Ms. Garcia's class went to the

_____.

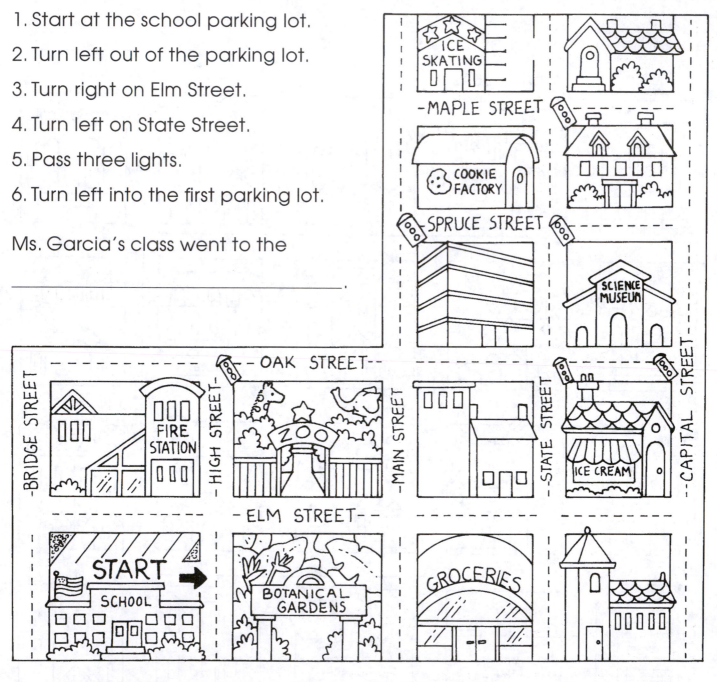

On the back of this paper, draw three things you think Ms. Garcia's class saw on their field trip.

Name _____ Date _____

Reach the Beach

Look at the map and read the directions. To find out which route Sandy took to the beach, trace the path with a crayon.

1. Go east out of the driveway.

2. Turn south at the first light.

3. Turn west on Ocean Street.

4. Go around the fountain, and turn south into the street.

5. Turn east into the parking lot.

Which parking lot did she park in? _____

N
W ← E
S

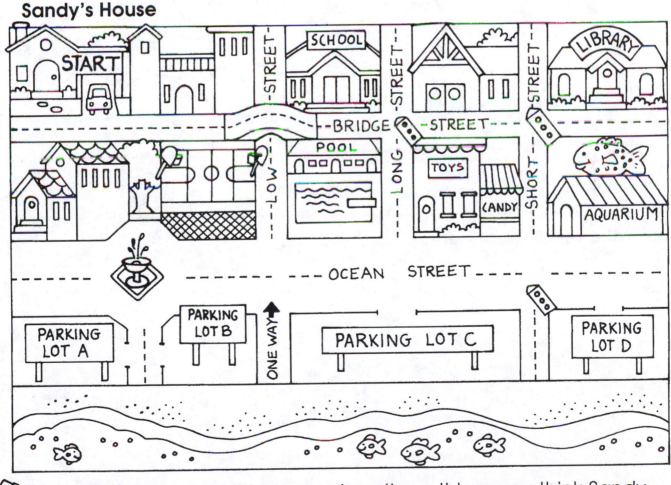

On the back of this paper, draw three things you think Sandy did or saw at the beach.

Teacher, I'm Done! ©2001 Creative Teaching Press

Name _____ Date _____

Ready Teddy!

Follow each step to draw a teddy bear.

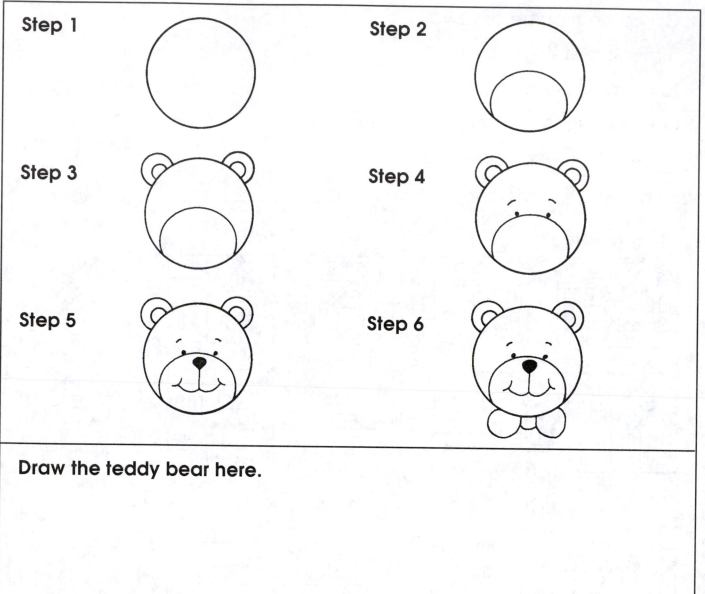

Step 1

Step 2

Step 3

Step 4

Step 5

Step 6

Draw the teddy bear here.

Teacher, I'm Done! ©2001 Creative Teaching Press

Name _____ Date _____

Just Ducky

Follow each step to draw a duck.

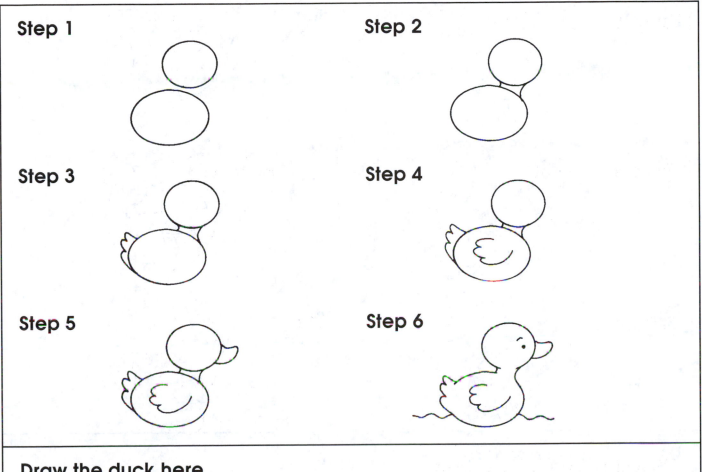

Step 1

Step 2

Step 3

Step 4

Step 5

Step 6

Draw the duck here.

Let's Draw!

Name _____ Date _____

Dino-Mite Dinosaur

Follow each step to draw a dinosaur.

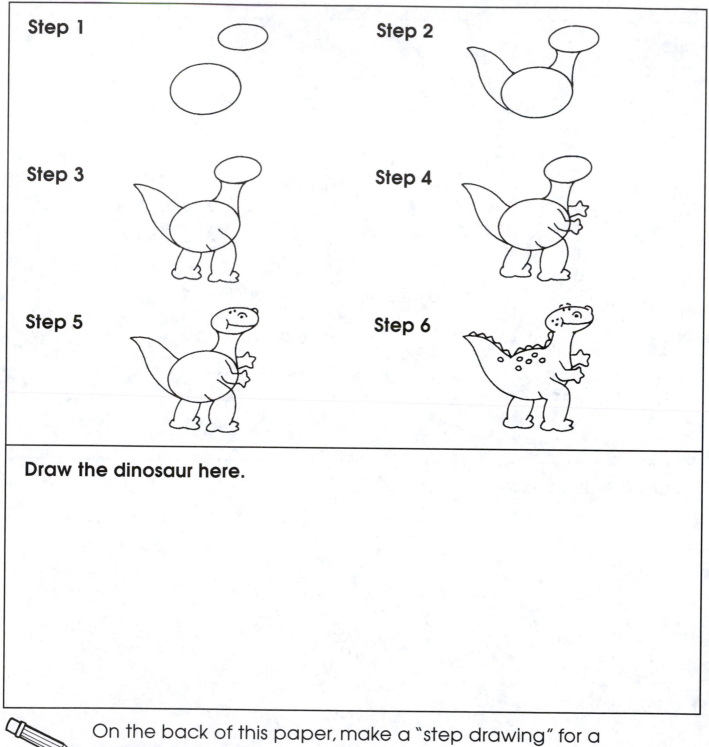

Step 1

Step 2

Step 3

Step 4

Step 5

Step 6

Draw the dinosaur here.

On the back of this paper, make a "step drawing" for a friend to complete.

Teacher, I'm Done! ©2001 Creative Teaching Press

Clowning Around

Follow the strings to see who is holding each balloon. Write the number of the balloon below each clown. Color the picture.

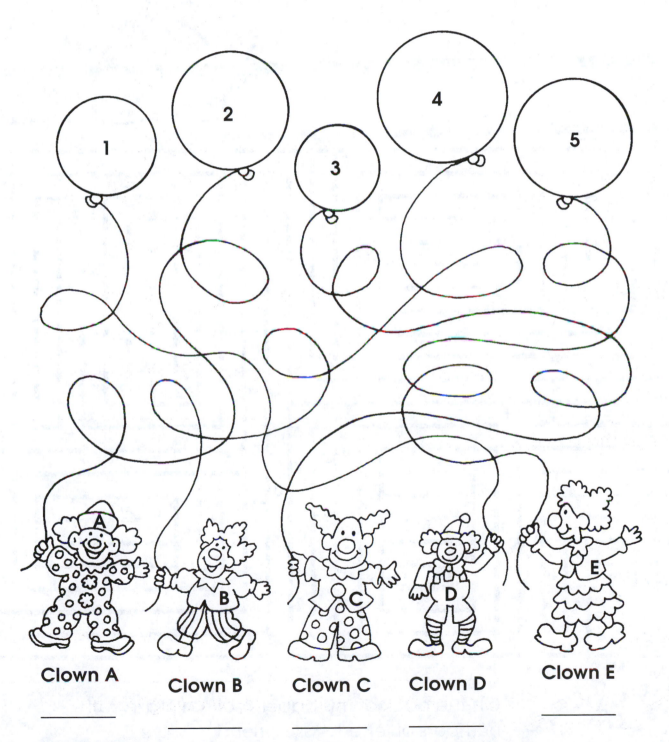

Clown A _____

Clown B _____

Clown C _____

Clown D _____

Clown E _____

Name _____ Date _____

A-Mazing Letters

Use a pencil to follow the alphabet through
the maze to help the bear find the honey.

On the back of this paper, make a maze with
numbers or letters. Ask a friend to solve it.

Name _____ Date _____

Mitten Maze

Use a pencil to follow this sentence through the maze and get the child to the correct pair of mittens: **I wear mittens on cold winter days.**

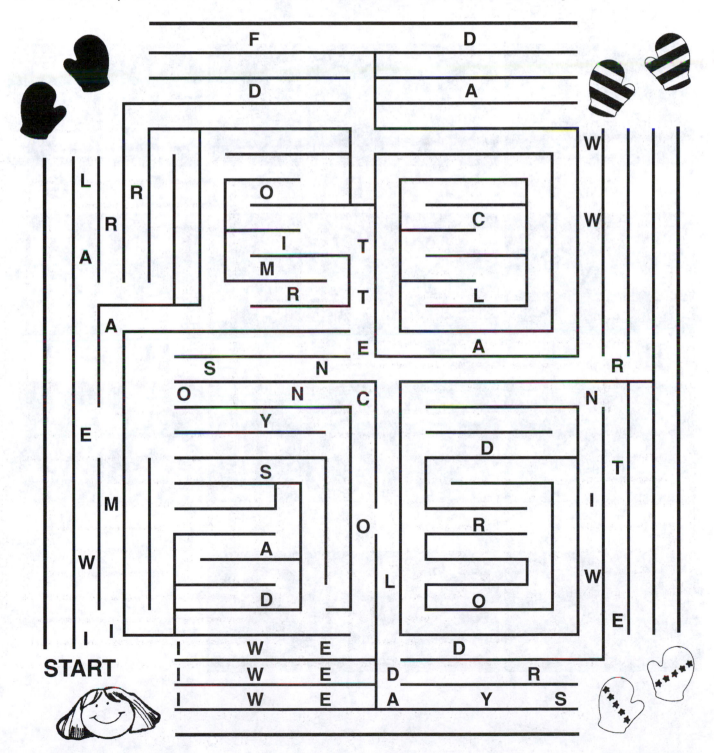

START

Teacher, I'm Done! ©2001 Creative Teaching Press

Name _____ Date _____

Braille Mail

Look at the Braille letters below. Real Braille uses raised dots. People who can't see read Braille by feeling each set of dots. Use Braille to break the code on pages 89 and 90.

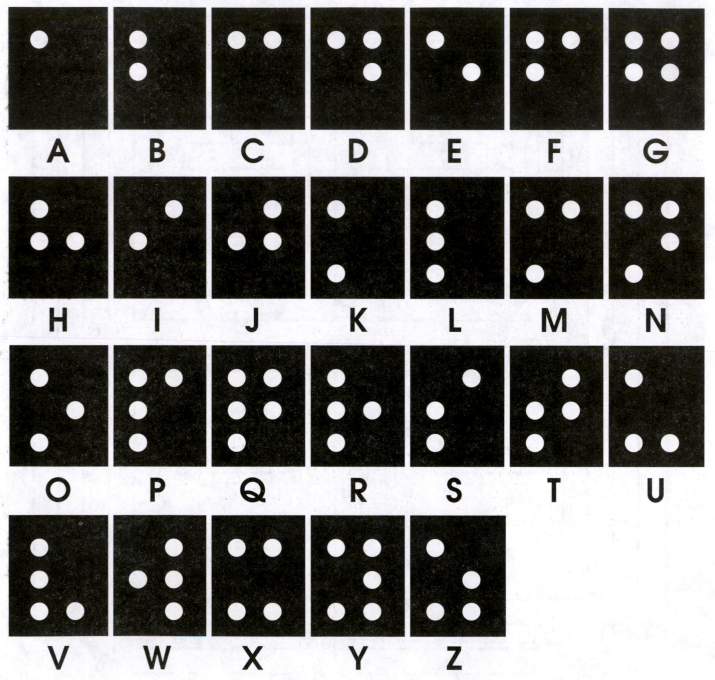

Teacher, I'm Done! ©2001 Creative Teaching Press

Name _____ Date _____

Braille Mail 1

Use the code on page 88 to solve the puzzle below. Write a letter under each set of dots.

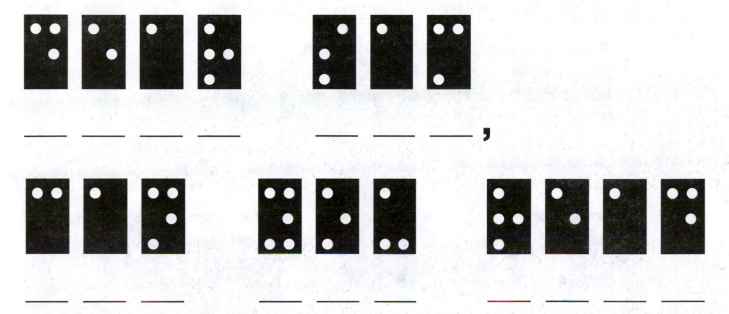

___ ___ ___ ___   ___ ___ ___,

___ ___ ___   ___ ___ ___   ___ ___ ___ ___

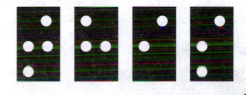

___ ___ ___ ___ **?**

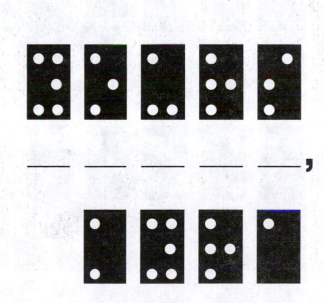

___ ___ ___ ___ ___,

___ ___ ___ ___

Name _____ Date _____

Braille Mail 2

Use the code on page 88 to solve the puzzle below. Write a letter under each set of dots.

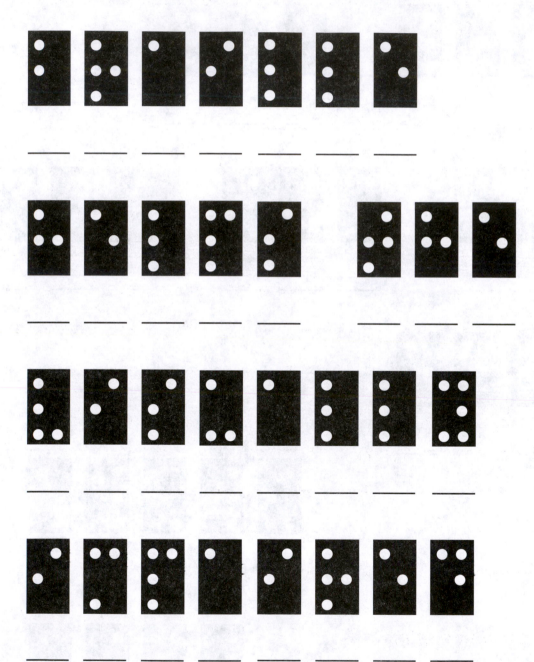

_____

_____   _____

_____

_____

 On the back of this paper, create your own secret code.
Make a puzzle for a friend to solve.

Name _____   Date _____

Morse Code Message

Morse code is used to send messages over telegraphs and radios. Look at the Morse code below. Use this code to solve the puzzles on pages 92 and 93.

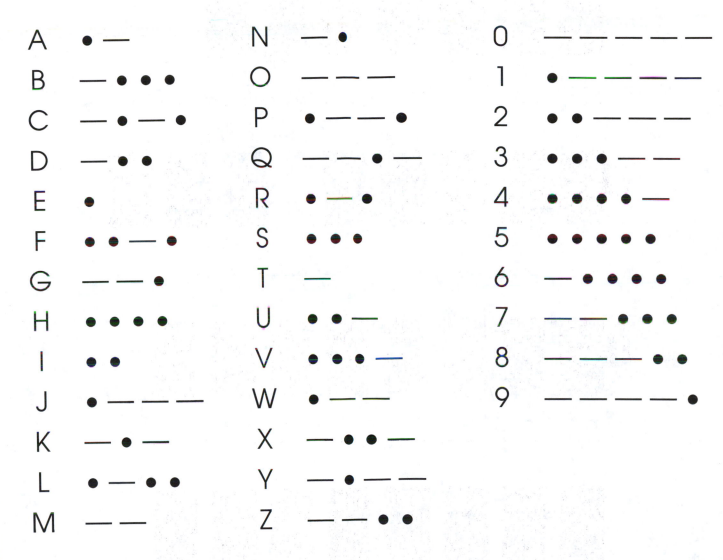

Space between letters   /
Space between words   //

Name _____ Date _____

Morse Code Message 1

Use the Morse code on page 91 to solve the puzzle below.
Write a letter in each box.

Teacher, I'm Done! ©2001 Creative Teaching Press

Date _____

Message 2

ge 91 to solve the puzzle below.

— — / • • — / • / • — • • //
□   □   □   □

— / • — • / • • • / • //
   □   □   □

• / — • / — / • / — • • //
□   □   □   □   □

/ • — • / • • • / • //
□   □   □

• // • • / — • //
□   □

/ • — — — —
        □

...her Morse code

---

3 + 3 = 6
4 + 4 = 8
2 + 4 =
9. 3 + 4
10. 1 +

3
7
= 5
2 = 5
4 = 5
5 = 9

+ 4 + 3 = 11
+ 9 + 5 = 18
7 + 9 + 6 = 22
3 + 7 + 1 = 11
9 + 9 + 5 = 23
8 + 1 + 5 = 14
4 + 1 + 7 = 12

...lored according

(page 37)

Write (page 38)

Answer Key

Animals (page 5)
dog, dot, cot, cat
pig, pin, pen, hen
rat, bat, bag, bug

More Animals (page 6)
hen, hem, ham, ram
cat, car, jar, jay
bee, bet, bat, cat

Transportation (page 7)
car, cab, cub, sub
jet, vet, vat, van
bus, but, bet, jet

Things in the Kitchen (page 8)
nut, hut, hat, ham
jar, car, can, pan
mat, rat, rag, rug

Silent *e* Words (page 9)
hive, five, fire, tire
robe, rose, hose, hole
gate, game, came, cake

More Silent *e* Words (page 10)
bike, bake, cake, cape
cave, cane, cone, bone
take, rake, race, rice

Pages 11–16
Pictures will vary.

Goat's Clues (page 17)
1. coat   2. boat   3. moat
4. throat   5. float

Kitty's Clues (page 18)
1. cart   2. coat   3. tack
4. crate   5. patch   6. carrot

Bunny's Clues (page 19)
1. hear   2. fear   3. tears
4. heart   5. earn   6. early
7. earth   8. learn

Pages 20–24
Words will vary.

Add It Up! (page 25)

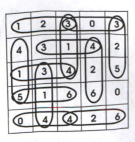

The Sum of It (page 26)

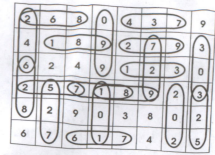

Really "Sum-thing"! (page 27)

Subtract It! (page 28)

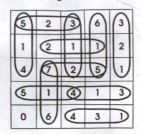

Find the Difference (page 29)

More Minuses (page 30)

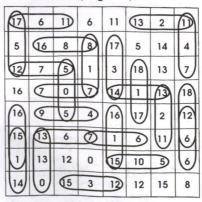

Four Square (page 31)
1. $1 + 2 = 3$
2. $3 + 2 = 5$
3. $1 + 1 = 2$
4. $1 + 4 = 5$
5. $2 + 2 = 4$

Six Square (page 3?)
1. $0 + 4 = 4$
2. $5 + 5 = 10$
3. $1 + 3 = 4$
4. $4 + 2 = 6$
5. $5 + 3 = 8$
6. $3 + 4 = 7$

Nine Square (?. 4?)
1. $5 + 2 + 7 =$ 9. 4
2. $8 + 8 + 6 =$ 10.
3. $8 + 6 + 4 =$ 11
4. $4 + 2 + 9 =$ 12
5. $5 + 9 + =$ 1
6. $1 + 5 + =$
7. $2 + 7 = 11$

Pages ?–36
Picture should be c
to directions.

Write the Number (

Add and

94

Name _____ Date _____

Morse Code Message 2

Use the Morse code on page 91 to solve the puzzle below.
Write a letter in each box.

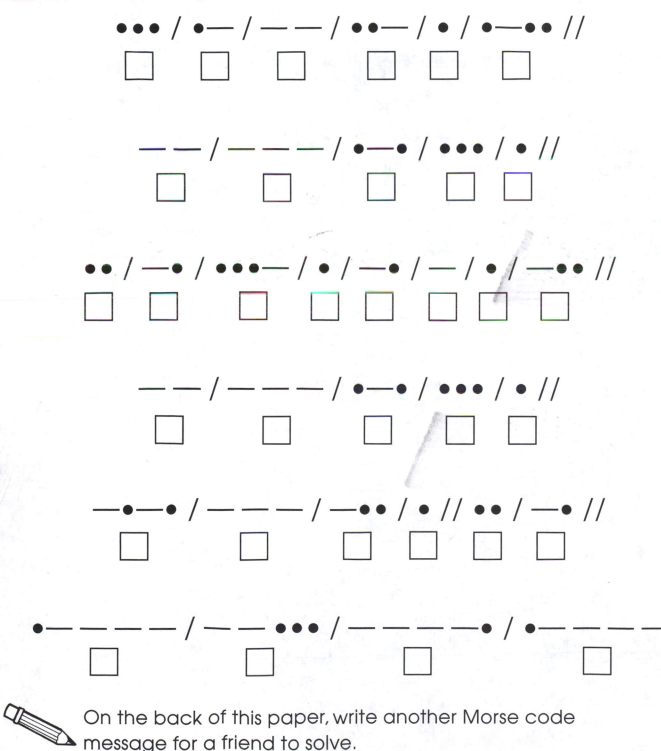

On the back of this paper, write another Morse code
message for a friend to solve.

Answer Key

Animals (page 5)
dog, dot, cot, cat
pig, pin, pen, hen
rat, bat, bag, bug

More Animals (page 6)
hen, hem, ham, ram
cat, car, jar, jay
bee, bet, bat, cat

Transportation (page 7)
car, cab, cub, sub
jet, vet, vat, van
bus, but, bet, jet

Things in the Kitchen (page 8)
nut, hut, hat, ham
jar, car, can, pan
mat, rat, rag, rug

Silent e Words (page 9)
hive, five, fire, tire
robe, rose, hose, hole
gate, game, came, cake

More Silent e Words (page 10)
bike, bake, cake, cape
cave, cane, cone, bone
take, rake, race, rice

Pages 11–16
Pictures will vary.

Goat's Clues (page 17)
1. coat   2. boat   3. moat
4. throat   5. float

Kitty's Clues (page 18)
1. cart   2. coat   3. tack
4. crate   5. patch   6. carrot

Bunny's Clues (page 19)
1. hear   2. fear   3. tears
4. heart   5. earn   6. early
7. earth   8. learn

Pages 20–24
Words will vary.

Add It Up! (page 25)

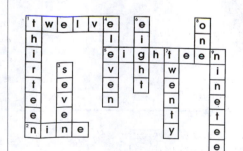

The Sum of It (page 26)

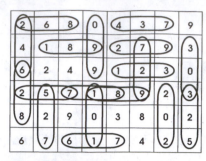

Really "Sum-thing"! (page 27)

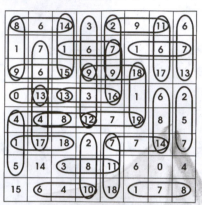

Subtract It! (page 28)

Find the Difference (page 29)

More Minuses (page 30)

Four Square (page 31)
1. 1 + 2 = 3   6. 3 + 3 = 6
2. 3 + 2 = 5   7. 4 + 4 = 8
3. 1 + 1 = 2   8. 2 + 4 = 6
4. 1 + 4 = 5   9. 3 + 4 = 7
5. 2 + 2 = 4   10. 1 + 3 = 4

Six Square (page 32)
1. 0 + 4 = 4   7. 2 + 1 = 3
2. 5 + 5 = 10   8. 2 + 5 = 7
3. 1 + 3 = 4   9. 0 + 5 = 5
4. 4 + 2 = 6   10. 3 + 2 = 5
5. 5 + 3 = 8   11. 1 + 4 = 5
6. 3 + 4 = 7   12. 4 + 5 = 9

Nine Square (page 33)
1. 5 + 2 + 7 = 14   8. 4 + 4 + 3 = 11
2. 8 + 8 + 6 = 22   9. 4 + 9 + 5 = 18
3. 8 + 6 + 4 = 18   10. 7 + 9 + 6 = 22
4. 4 + 2 + 9 = 15   11. 3 + 7 + 1 = 11
5. 5 + 9 + 1 = 15   12. 9 + 9 + 5 = 23
6. 1 + 5 + 1 = 7   13. 8 + 1 + 5 = 14
7. 2 + 7 + 2 = 11   14. 4 + 1 + 7 = 12

Pages 34–36
Pictures should be colored according to directions.

Write the Number (page 37)

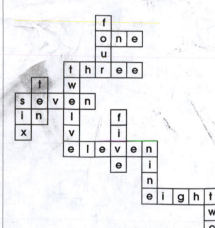

Add and Write (page 38)

Teacher, I'm Done! ©2001 Creative Teaching Press

Subtract and Write (page 39)

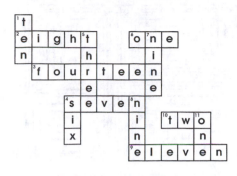

Desert Trail (page 40)

1. 3, _4_, 5, 6, 7, 8, _9_, 10, _11_, _12_, 13
   Rule: +1
2. 4, 6, _8_, 10, 12, _14_, 16, _18_, 20
   Rule: +2
3. 3, 6, _9_, 12, 15, _18_, 21, _24_
   Rule: +3
4. 5, 10, _15_, 20, 25, _30_, 35, _40_
   Rule: +5

Hiking Trail (page 41)

1. 2, 5, _8_, 11, 14, _17_, _20_, 23
   Rule: +3
2. 40, 35, _30_, 25, 20, 15, _10_, 5, _0_
   Rule: −5
3. 20, 18, _16_, 14, 12, _10_, 8, 6, _4_
   Rule: −2
4. 85, 75, _65_, _55_, 45, 35, _25_, 15, _5_
   Rule: −10

Pet Paths (page 42)

1. 5, 9, 13, _17_, 21, _25_, 29, _33_, 37
   Rule: +4
2. 25, 22, _19_, 16, 13, _10_, 7, _4_, 1
   Rule: −3
3. 27, 35, 43, _51_, 59, 67, _75_, 83, _91_
   Rule: +8
4. 69, 57, _45_, 33, _21_, 9
   Rule: −12

Time for Recess (page 43)

1. girl backing down slide
2. upside-down bench
3. upside-down flag
4. swing without chains
5. girl in winter clothes
6. end of jump rope
7. roller skate
8. upside-down flower
9. upside-down 5
10. mismatched socks

Max's Messy Room (page 44)

1. bottomless bird cage
2. upside-down sign
3. floating pillow
4. bed leg missing
5. two-ended broom
6. only one sock
7. backward number 3 on clock

8. flowers
9. truck missing wheel
10. tree
11. plug in wall, no socket
12. missing lightbulb
13. rain cloud
14. picture on ceiling
15. upside-down curtains

Toy Store (page 45)

1. upside-down picture
2. phone door handle
3. sunglasses without lens
4. black piano keys
5. banana peel
6. teapot with two spouts
7. yo-yo with two strings
8. hippo's pencil tooth
9. doll's hand with four fingers
10. car missing wheel
11. child's mismatched sleeves
12. deflated football
13. upside-down purse
14. upside-down "sale" sign
15. bunny missing ear
16. jack-in-the-box's lightbulb head
17. upside-down plane
18. sled with wheels
19. backward 3 on cash register
20. cashier's mismatched sleeves

Sports Fan (page 46)

Row 1: football helmet
Row 2: tennis shoe
Row 3: vaulting horse
Row 4: basket

Get in Shape (page 47)

Row 1: present
Row 2: lunch box
Row 3: balloon
Row 4: sandwich

Think About It! (page 48)

Row 1: square, boy, long, Monday, dirt
Row 2: water, apple, bug, milk, candy
Row 3: boat, big, horse, skates, dark

Behind the Curtain (page 49)

Answer: horse

A Special Package (page 50)

Answer: sailboat

In the Sky (page 51)

Answer: meteor

Pat's Cats (page 52)

Pat's cats all have collars.

The Blobs (page 53)

Blobs all have two antennae and smiles.

Awesome Aces (page 54)

Awesome Aces all have three stripes, dark outlined tires, and drivers.

Happy Apples (page 55)

Crazy Cows (page 56)

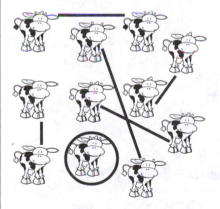

Tricky Totems (page 57)

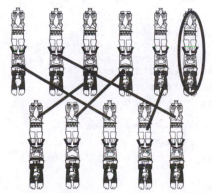

Find the Partners (page 58)

Flipped Partners (page 59)

Shadow to Shadow (page 60)

Pages 61–63
Pictures will vary.

Counting Triangles (page 64)
The first shape has 5 triangles.
The second shape has 8 triangles.

Counting Squares (page 65)
The first shape has 10 squares.
The second shape has 15 squares.

Counting Rectangles (page 66)
The shape has 14 rectangles.

Pages 67–72
Pictures will vary.

Pages 73–78
Answers will vary.

Mike's Market (page 79)
The shortest route is about 5 inches.

Field Trip Fun (page 80)
Ms. Garcia's class went to the ice skating rink.

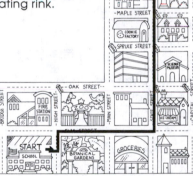

Reach the Beach (page 81)
She parked in Parking Lot B.

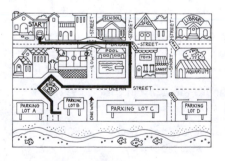

Pages 82–84
Pictures will vary.

Clowning Around (page 85)

Clown A: 2	Clown D: 1
Clown B: 4	Clown E: 5
Clown C: 3	

A-Mazing Letters (page 86)

Mitten Maze (page 87)

Braille Mail 1 (page 89)
Dear Sam,
Can you read this?
Yours,
Kyra

Braille Mail 2 (page 90)
Braille helps the visually impaired.

Morse Code Message 1 (page 92)
A common Morse code message is SOS.

Morse Code Message 2 (page 93)
Samuel Morse invented Morse code in 1791.